YOUR KNOWLEDGE HAS VALUE

- We will publish your bachelor's and master's thesis, essays and papers

- Your own eBook and book - sold worldwide in all relevant shops

- Earn money with each sale

Upload your text at www.GRIN.com and publish for free

Bibliographic information published by the German National Library:

The German National Library lists this publication in the National Bibliography; detailed bibliographic data are available on the Internet at http://dnb.dnb.de .

Imprint:

Copyright © 2017 GRIN Verlag
Print and binding: Books on Demand GmbH, Norderstedt Germany
ISBN: 9783346145505

This book at GRIN:

https://www.grin.com/document/536597

Florian Beyer

What is the Bootstrap Effect? Merger & Acquisition-Activities and their Influence on Stock Prices

GRIN Verlag

GRIN - Your knowledge has value

Since its foundation in 1998, GRIN has specialized in publishing academic texts by students, college teachers and other academics as e-book and printed book. The website www.grin.com is an ideal platform for presenting term papers, final papers, scientific essays, dissertations and specialist books.

Visit us on the internet:

http://www.grin.com/

http://www.facebook.com/grincom

http://www.twitter.com/grin_com

M&A activities' influence on stock prices

–

The bootstrap effect

Study Programme

Master of Business Administration (MBA)

.

Author:	Florian Beyer
Place, Date:	Hamburg, July 17, 2017

Table of contents

List of figures III

List of tables IV

List of abbreviations V

1 Introduction 1

2 Mergers & acquisitions at a glance 2

3 Mergers & acquisitions' influence on the share price 5

   3.1 Influence of takeover announcements 5

   3.2 Shareholder value approach 6

   3.3 Calculation of the shareholder value 8

4 The bootstrap effect 9

   4.1 Account of the bootstrap effect 10

   4.2 Appliance of the bootstrap effect 10

   4.3 Consequences for mergers and acquisitions 11

5 Conclusion 12

Annex V

   A-1: Weighted average cost of capital V

   A-2: Free cash flow VI

   A-3: Earnings per share and price-earnings ratio VII

Bibliography VIII

Internet bibliography X

List of figures

FIGURE 1: RAPPAPORT'S SHAREHOLDER VALUE NETWORK 7

List of tables

TABLE 1: EXEMPLARY CALCULATION OF THE BOOTSTRAP EFFECT·..........11

List of abbreviations

EBIT	Earnings before interest and taxes
EPS	Earnings per share
FCF	Free cash flow
M&A	Mergers and acquisitions
mn.	Million
NWC	Net working capital
P/E	Price-earnings ratio
R&D	Research and development
ROE	Return on equity
ROI	Return on investment
SG&A	Selling, general, and administrative
SHV	Shareholder value
SVN	Shareholder value network
tn.	Trillion
USD	US-Dollars
V	Value
WACC	Weighted average cost of capital

V

1 Introduction

In 2016, the global mergers and acquisitions (M&A) activities decreased by about 18 percent compared to 2015. Altogether, 17,369 deals with a value of 3.2 trillion (tn.) US-Dollars (USD) were performed.[1]

There are numerous reasons to invest and divest in inorganic growth. Organic growth has its limitations, thus acquiring competitors, growing vertically or horizontally as well as accessing new markets are strong motivators to do so. Growing a business is often linked with going public. The decision to be part of the stock market and to perform M&A influences an enterprise's value for various reasons. Therefore, this paper will examine the question: how do M&A activities influence a company's stock price and earnings per share (EPS), especially if the bootstrap effect occurs?

To approach this question, the first chapter gives a general overview of reasons, motivators, risks and benefits of M&A. Thereafter, the influence of M&A on a company's shareholder value and EPS is examined. Then, the bootstrap effect is explained and subsequently illustrated by an exemplary M&A transaction. Afterwards the risks and benefits of bootstrapping and M&A are analysed to consider its usefulness and influence on the share price and EPS.

---

[1] Mergermarket, "Global and regional M&A: Q1-Q4 2016," [http://www.mergermarket.com/pdf/MergermarketFinancialLeagueTableReport.Q42016.pdf], accessed April 2017, p. 3.

2 Mergers & acquisitions at a glance

There exist various forms and reasons for M&A. This chapter outlines a general overview of the different forms and investigates the reasons to perform M&A, examining its motives critically.

In M&A there are two roles the related companies are assigned to: the target and the acquirer.[2] The transaction is either a merger or an acquisition, also called takeover. A merger combines the acquirer and the target company, forming a new entity. Whereas an acquisition integrates the target in the acquiring company, resulting in the target's vanishing.[3] Depending on the direction of the transaction, three different forms of M&A can be distinguished:[4]

- Horizontal merger/acquisition
- Vertical merger/acquisition
- Conglomerate merger/acquisition

A horizontal merger is typically a transaction, in which the acquirer buys a target in the same industry e.g. a competitor. If the transaction's direction is aimed forward or backward in the production chain e.g. a car manufacturer buys a car component manufacturer, the business transaction is called vertical merger. The merge of two unrelated businesses in regards to the industry is a conglomerate transaction.[5]

The major motivators to merge are the underlying expectation of synergies and the assumption of managers, that the market undervalues the target firm. The second motivator's main financial gain is to sell the components of the target firm at a higher price than the acquisition price was. The first motivator's outcome is a higher value (V) of the amalgamation of both firms, due to synergies according to the formula.[6]

$$V_{A+B} > V_A + V_B \qquad (1)$$

Therefore, synergies are:[7]

---

[2] Berk, J., and Peter DeMarzo, *Corporate Finance*, 3rd ed. (Boston, MA: Pearson, 2014), p. 931.
[3] Pike, Richard, and Bill Neale, *Corporate Finance and Investment: Decisions & Strategies*, 5th ed. (Harlow: Financial Times Prentice Hall, 2006), pp. 542-543.
[4] Berk, J., and Peter DeMarzo, *Corporate Finance*, p. 933.
[5] Brealey, Richard A., Myers, Stewart C., and Alan J. Marcus, *Fundamentals of Corporate Finance*, 3rd ed. (McGraw-Hill Higher Education, 2001), p. 572.
[6] Pike, Richard, and Bill Neale, *Corporate Finance and Investment: Decisions & Strategies*, p. 548.
[7] Ross, Stephen A., Westerfield, Randolph W., and Jaffrey Jaffe, *Corporate Finance*, 6th ed. (Boston, MA: McGraw-Hill/Irwin, 2003), p.823.

$$\text{Synergy} = V_{A+B} - (V_A - V_B) \qquad\qquad (2)$$

Formula 1 assumes that the values of firm A (V_A) and firm B (V_B) are increased due to synergies if they are merged and create firm AB (V_{A+B}). Consequently, formula 2 defines the created synergy as the subtraction of the firms' single values before the merger from the combined firm's value.

Synergies occur in different extent and forms. Economies of scale and scope are resulting in savings e.g. for economies of scale, the higher volume of the merged firms needs a larger amount of input goods to create products, thus the unit costs are cut.[8] There are strategic benefits, which create new opportunities in regards to technological chances e.g. Procter & Gamble acquiring Charmin Paper Company, resulting in hygiene products created out of the interrelation of the companies.[9] Moreover, this is economies of scope or the combination of complementary resources, because the combination of both company's resources resulted in savings and new opportunities.[10] Besides these synergies, monopoly and efficiency gains as well as acquired expertise are accompanying the merger of two firms. Monopoly gains are created by eliminating rivalry within an industry, when one rival acquires the other. Efficiency is increased when duplicated structures of both firms are consolidated or a more efficient board replaces the former management.[11]

A principal argument for an M&A transaction, especially for a conglomerate takeover is diversification. Positive aspects of diversification are an increased debt capacity and decreased borrowing costs due to the lower risk of bankruptcy.[12]

Especially, cash rich firms with high surplus are diversifying[13] despite the fact that investors do not pay a premium for diversified firms or long-term value is created.[14] Instead of running the risk to invest in a non-value-creating acquisition, it is preferable to invest in internal growth or, if there is no opportunity to invest internally, a return of cash in forms of dividends or share buybacks.[15] A major reason for diversification is risk reduction due to a distribution

---

[8] Berk, J., and Peter DeMarzo, *Corporate Finance*, p. 935.
[9] Ross, Stephen A., Westerfield, Randolph W., and Jaffrey Jaffe, *Corporate Finance*, p. 825.
[10] Brealey, Richard A., Myers, Stewart C., and Alan J. Marcus, *Fundamentals of Corporate Finance*, pp. 574-575.
[11] Berk, J., and Peter DeMarzo, *Corporate Finance*, pp. 935-936.
[12] Ibid., p. 938.
[13] Ross, Stephen A., Westerfield, Randolph W., and Jaffrey Jaffe, *Corporate Finance*, p. 834.
[14] Brealey, Richard A., Myers, Stewart C., and Franklin Allen, *Principles of Corporate Finance*, 10th ed. (Boston, MA: McGraw-Hill/Irwin, 2011), p. 798.
[15] Rappaport, Alfred, "Ten Ways to Create Shareholder Value," *Harvard Business Review*, September 2006, https://hbr.org/2006/09/ten-ways-to-create-shareholder-value, accessed July 2017.

of the risk. Shareholders are able to reach risk reduction much easier if they buy shares of different firms. They diversify their own portfolio of shares to reduce risk, thus the diversification by an acquisition has no beneficial effect on shareholders. Moreover, the acquisition could possibly reduce the shareholder value due to the merger costs and increased costs of running a diversified business.[16]

---

[16] Berk, J., and Peter DeMarzo, *Corporate Finance*, p. 938.

3   Mergers & acquisitions' influence on the share price

Besides the mentioned economic motives for M&A, there are several managerial motivations to perform takeovers. Generally, managers of larger firms are usually experience compensation based advantages, thus growing the company inorganically increases the managers' salaries faster compared to organic growth.[17] This could lead to a conflict of interests, because managers of large firms earn more money but hold very little fractions of the company's stocks. Therefore, the risk of a financially inefficient merger has more influence on the shareholder value than on the manager's compensation. Managers' overconfidence in their own abilities to integrate every takeover successfully could lead to a decrease of shareholder value, but could cause a gain for the managers' income.[18] Besides the increasing company size to increasing manager income relation, sometimes the compensation is based on stock performance e.g. EPS. This can cause managers to merge firms, despite the fact that there is any economic growth or value creation but an increase in the EPS or even share price.[19] This so-called "bootstrap effect" occurs when the investors respectively the market is fooled and overvalues the company.[20] This effect is discussed later on.

3.1   Influence of takeover announcements

A company planning to take over another firm has to announce the tender offer publicly. The sheer announcement has a traceable effect on both companies' share prices. The share price of large acquirers in a merger decrease on average when the offer is announced, particularly if the target is a publicly listed company (one reason may be the mentioned conflict of interests).[21,22] Literature and studies concerning this topic are not overall consistent. However, target companies' shareholders involved in mergers or takeovers are gaining significant cumulative abnormal returns, sometimes even prior to an announcement due to leaked information.[23]

---

[17]   Pike, Richard, and Bill Neale, *Corporate Finance and Investment: Decisions & Strategies*, p. 551.
[18]   Berk, J., and Peter DeMarzo, *Corporate Finance*, p. 940.
[19]   Pike, Richard, and Bill Neale, *Corporate Finance and Investment: Decisions & Strategies*, p. 551.
[20]   Brealey, Richard A., Myers, Stewart C., and Franklin Allen, *Principles of Corporate Finance*, p. 799.
[21]   Berk, J., and Peter DeMarzo, *Corporate Finance*, pp. 939-941.
[22]   Wong, Anson, and Kui Yin Cheung, "The Effects of Merger and Acquisition Announcements on the Security Prices of Bidding Firms and Target Firms in Asia," International Journal of Economics and Finance 1, no. 2 (August 2009), p. 275.
[23]   McGowan, Carl B., and Zunaidah Sulong, "A Note On The Effect Of M&A Announcements On Stock Price Behavior And Financial Performance Changes: The Case Of Arab Malaysian Bank Berhad And Hong Leong Bank Berhad," *International Business & Economics Research Journal* 7, no. 9 (September 2008), p. 22.

A study and extensive literature review of Kumar and Panneerselvam[24] found positive abnormal gains for both firms involved in the transaction, especially in the period encompassing the announcement. Highest positive gains have the target firms included in a merger followed by the acquirers. They are followed by the gains of acquirers involved in an acquisition transaction. This is in contrast to the before mentioned decrease[25], but can be associated to different data sets respective analysed periods and firms. Averaged, M&A are value-creating activities but stockholders of the acquirer receive more gains compared to stockholders of the target firms in acquisitions. The outcome for mergers is vice versa.[26]

Concluding, M&A transactions are potentially beneficial for shareholders, but it depends on each transaction's circumstances and managers involved. The announcements and linked share price variations are opportunities for risk arbitrageurs[27] but long-term value-oriented management better focuses on post-merger integration and a successful realisation of the anticipated synergies to create shareholder value.[28]

3.2 Shareholder value approach

The enterprise value of a firm is calculated as the market value of equity plus the debt minus the cash out of marketable securities. The enterprise value aims to assess the value of the business' assets.[29] This balance sheet based calculation is not suitable to calculate shareholder value, because book values are not market values. Furthermore, an investor respectively shareholder is interested in future profits and surplus of the company. The expectation is future positive cash flows in forms of increased stock price and dividends.[30]

The shareholder value approach (SVN) is a management approach developed by Rappaport to maximise shareholder value.

This approach is based on discounted cash flow calculation of investments, as often used for net present value calculation. Rappaport[31] extends this calculation to value a business or parts of it to the strategic planning and controlling of management decisions. Therefore, the approach evaluates both, investments in forms of acquisitions and strategic decisions of the

---

[24] Kumar, B. Rajesh, and S. Panneerselvam, "Mergers, Acquisitions and Wealth Creation: A Comparative Study in the Indian Context," *IIMB Management Review* 21, no. 3 (2009), pp. 241-242.

[25] Brealey, Richard A., Myers, Stewart C., and Franklin Allen, *Principles of Corporate Finance*, p. 813.

[26] Ibid., p.

[27] Berk, J., and Peter DeMarzo, *Corporate Finance*, p. 943.

[28] Rappaport, Alfred, "Ten Ways to Create Shareholder Value".

[29] Berk, J., and Peter DeMarzo, *Corporate Finance*, p. 28.

[30] Prangenberg, Arno, Müller, Matthias, and Manuela Aldenhoff, "Der Shareholder-Value-Ansatz," *Arbeitshilfen für Aufsichtsräte* 9, 4th ed. (Düsseldorf: Hans-Böckler-Stiftung, 2005), p. 9.

[31] Lohr, Burkhard, *Bewertung bauausführender Unternehmen: Ein ganzheitliches entscheidungsorientiertes Konzept* (Munich: Herbert Utz Verlag, 2001), p. 189.

management, contributions to shareholder value. It is an ongoing company valuation and success monitoring.[32] Figure 1 shows the shareholder value network and the influence of management decisions on value drivers, which contribute to the valuation components ultimately creating shareholder value.

Figure 1: Rappaport's shareholder value network[33]

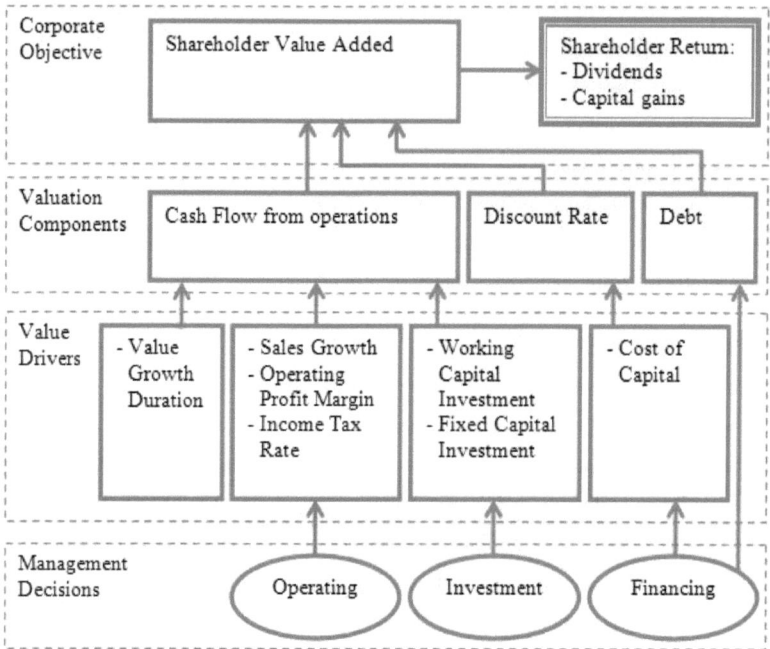

The network is based on the management dicisions concerning operations, investment and financing, which are conducive to value creation and result in the value drivers.

The value growth duration is the period where estimated returns will surpass the cost of capital. Value drivers related to the operating and investment as well as the value growth duration are contributing to the cash flows from operations.[34] Wheras, financing creates debts and at a certain cost of capital to fund the investment influences the discount rate.[35] The

---

[32] Ibid.

[33] Graphic based on Rappaport, Alfred, *Creating Shareholder Value: A Guide For Managers and Investors* (New York, NY: The Free Press, 1998), p. 56.

[34] Giurca, Vasilecu Laura, "New Approaches On Shareholders Value Of A Firm," Faculty of Economy and Business Administration, University of Craiova, 2007, p. 663.

[35] Lohr, Burkhard, *Bewertung bauausführender Unternehmen: Ein ganzheitliches entscheidungsorientiertes Konzept*, p. 190.

outcome is shareholder value added in forms of devidends or capital gains due to increased share prices. The SVN is the fundament for several other discounted cash flow methods to calculate companies' success in forms of excess profits e.g. economic value added by Steward and Bennett.[36]

3.3   Calculation of the shareholder value

The shareholder value of a company is calculated when the market value of debt is subtracted from the total business value. The total business value is the addition of the summation of the present value of future cash flows for a projected period, the residual value of future cash flows from a period following the projected period and discounted at the weighted average cost of capital (WACC).[37] The account corresponds with the discounted cash flow method.[38] Future cash flows incorporate the present value of capital and the general business risks.[39] Several value drivers as depicted in Figure 1 influence the cash flows. They are called free cash flows (FCF) as they are free to be distributed to shareholders.[40] The residual value is defined as the price a fixed asset can be sold for at the end of its projected economic life. Therefore, cash flows can arise after the projected period. The WACC is the average cost of debt and equity.[41] It represents the opportunity costs of the assets in use and is market driven.[42]

The WACC is denoted as r_{WACC} and its calculation is found in annex A-1. The future free cash flow of a period is denoted as FCF_t and calculated in annex A-2. According to the previous description the shareholder value (SHV) is calculated as follows:[43,44]

---

[36]   Wellner, Kai-Uwe, *Shareholder-Value und seine Weiterentwicklung zum Market Adapted Shareholder Value Approach* (Marburg: Tectum Verlag, 2001), p. 77.
[37]   Pandey, M., and D. Arora, "Shareholder Value Analysis: A Review," *International Journal of Science and Research* 4, no. 5 (May 2015), p. 2130.
[38]   Chari, Latha, and R. P. Mohanty, "Understanding Value Creation: The Shareholder Value Perspective," *LBS Journal of Management & Research* 7, no. 1 and 2 (2009), p. 21.
[39]   Wellner, Kai-Uwe, *Shareholder-Value und seine Weiterentwicklung zum Market Adapted Shareholder Value Approach*, p. 65.
[40]   Chari, Latha, and R. P. Mohanty, "Understanding Value Creation: The Shareholder Value Perspective," p. 21.
[41]   Berk, J., and Peter DeMarzo, *Corporate Finance*, p. 285.
[42]   Pandey, M., and D. Arora, "Shareholder Value Analysis: A Review," p. 2131.
[43]   Wellner, Kai-Uwe, *Shareholder-Value und seine Weiterentwicklung zum Market Adapted Shareholder Value Approach*, p. 72.
[44]   Gantenbein, P. and M. Gehrig. "Moderne Unternehmensbewertung - Bewertungsziel mit Methodenmix erreichen." *Der Schweizer Treuhänder* 9 (2007), p. 608.

$$SHV = \sum_{t=1}^{T} \frac{FCF_t}{(1 + r_{WACC})^t} + \frac{CV_T}{(1 + r_{WACC})^T} - D_C$$

(3)

FCF$_t$ = free cash flow in period t

r$_{WACC}$ = weighted average cost of capital

D$_C$ = value of debt capital

CV$_T$ = continuing value (residual value)

The SHV calculation's foundation on the discounted cash flow is an accurate representation in contrast to static accounting numbers suchlike the EPS, price-earnings multiples, return in investment (ROI) or return on equity (ROE). Main reasons for this are the possibly alternative accounting methods, which were used to calculate them as well as the exclusion of investment requirements and the time value of money.[45] The SHV calculation mainly depends on a reliable and realistic estimation of the future cash flows.[46] Nevertheless, FCF is difficult to manipulate, internationally comparable and exactly regards the time of investments and distributed dividends and therefore the changes in working capital. This change in working capital is ignored by accounting numbers like the EPS. Thus, an earnings growth is not reliably related to an increased shareholder value or return in forms of dividends or higher share price.[47] The bootstrap effect emphasises this unreliability on EPS as an indicator for SHV creation. SHV's long-term orientation and generality fits to a reliable business performance indicator.

4 The bootstrap effect

M&A transactions can cause earnings growth without creating economic value. This accounting trick is based on the EPS and price-earnings ratio (P/E) and is referred to as the Bootstrap Effect (or bootstrapping, bootstrap or chain letter game).[48]

---

[45] Rappaport, Alfred, *Creating Shareholder Value*, pp. 13-14.
[46] Wellner, Kai-Uwe, *Shareholder-Value und seine Weiterentwicklung zum Market Adapted Shareholder Value Approach*, p. 66.
[47] Rappaport, Alfred, *Creating Shareholder Value*, pp. 20-21.
[48] Brealey, Richard A., Myers, Stewart C., and Franklin Allen, *Principles of Corporate Finance*, pp. 798-799.

4.1 Account of the bootstrap effect

There are two conditions, which must be met leading to the occurrence of the effect. First, the transactions payment must be a stock swap, where the acquiring company pays with shares instead of cash or other forms of payment.[49] Second, the acquiring company must have a higher P/E than the target company. Therefore, a high growth company acquires a low growth company, actually resulting in a decrease in growth rate for the combined entity.[50]

This transaction can increase the EPS, but should not increase the share price neither it should increase the short-term earnings due to a correction through a lower future earnings growth.[51] If the market is fooled or investors are misled by potential synergies, they expect the same P/E for the post-merger company as for the acquirer. The accounting with the premerger P/E leads to a higher market valuation of the post-merger company.

Efficient markets will regulate this and bootstrapping is not possible, but this takes a certain period. Thus, the acquiring company has a benefit out of merging with low performing companies to increase EPS until the market realises that no economic value is created.[52] Therefore, it is not possible to evaluate the benefits of the merger by focusing on the acquiring firm's earnings.[53] This tactic was used in the 1960's merger wave, which was characterised by conglomerate mergers[54] and rarely occurs in today's transactions.[55]

4.2 Appliance of the bootstrap effect

According to the previous chapter, the bootstrap effect influences the post-merger valuation of the company if the transaction is a stock swap. Furthermore, the acquiring company (company A) must have a higher P/E than the target company (company B). The exchange ratio for the stock swap is one share of company A equals two shares of company B. Table 1 shows the effect of bootstrapping and the influence of the incorrectly and correctly calculated P/E. Calculations for the EPS and P/E are in annex A-3.

---

49 Ibid., pp. 575-576.
50 Berk, J., and Peter DeMarzo, *Corporate Finance*, p. 939.
51 Brealey, Richard A., Myers, Stewart C., and Alan J. Marcus, *Fundamentals of Corporate Finance*, p. 577.
52 Gaughan, Patrick A., *Mergers, Acquisitions and Corporate Restructuring*, 3rd ed. (New York, John Wiley & Sons, 2002), pp. 539-542.
53 Berk, J., and Peter DeMarzo, *Corporate Finance*, p. 939.
54 Gaughan, Patrick A., *Mergers, Acquisitions and Corporate Restructuring*, pp. 539-540.
55 Brealey, Richard A., Myers, Stewart C., and Franklin Allen, *Principles of Corporate Finance*, p. 800.

Table 1: Exemplary calculation of the bootstrap effect[56,57]

	Pre-merger		Post-merger Company A	
	Company A	Company B	Unweighted P/E ratio	Weighted P/E ratio
EPS	1 USD	1 USD	1,20 USD	1,20 USD
Price per share	20 USD	10 USD	24 USD	20 USD
P/E	20	10	20	~ 16,67
Number of shares	100 mn.[58]	50 mn.	125 mn.	125 mn.
Total earnings	100 mn. USD	50 mn. USD	150 mn.	150 mn.
Total value	2 bn. USD	0,5 bn. USD	3 bn. USD	2,5 bn. USD

Table 1 shows the effect of an unweighted P/E and the influence on the share price and total market value of the business. The number of shares is reduced due to the stock swap and underlying exchange rate. The overall total earnings are the combination of both companies. The EPS is calculated based on the total earnings and number of shares, but the P/E is different.

If the bootstrapping effect is not detected the post-merger business has gained 500 mn. USD despite the fact that no economic value was added. Correctly calculated by the weighted P/E, the post-merger company is worth the same as the single total business values of the pre-merger companies.

4.3 Consequences for mergers and acquisitions

Besides the high number of M&A transactions, the criteria to verify the bootstrap effect make it difficult to find a real life example. Several mergers were investigated by the author but were not approved due to mismatched criteria for bootstrapping. The AmeriSource-Bergen merger was declined, because there were anticipated real synergies.[59,60] Several of the failed

---

[56] Ross, Stephen A., Westerfield, Randolph W., and Jaffrey Jaffe, *Corporate Finance*, p. 834.

[57] CFA Institute, "Chapter 10 – Mergers and Acquisitions," PowerPoint presentation, 2013, https://www.cfainstitute.org/learning/products/publications/inv/Documents/corporate_finance_chapter10.ppt x, accessed July 2017.

[58] Abbreviation for million.

[59] AmerisourceBergen, "SEC Filings – AmerisourceBergen," http://www.amerisourcebergen.net/investor/phoenix.zhtml?c=61181&p=irol-SECText&TEXT=aHR0cDovL2FwaS50ZW5rd2l6YXJkLmNvbS9maWxpbmcueG1sP2lwYWdlPTE0NDY3MTYmRFNFUT0wJlNFUT0wJlNRREVTYz1TRUNUSU9OX0VOVElSSRSZzdWJzaWQ9WQ9NTc%3d, accessed June 2017.

[60] Reckard, E. Scott, and Leslie Earnest, "Bergen Agrees to Be Acquired by AmeriSource in $2.3-Billion Deal," *Los Angeles Times*, March 20, 2001, http://articles.latimes.com/2001/mar/20/business/fi-40082, accessed July 2017.

M&A transactions listed in the CB Insights article[61] were examined but failed to match either the criteria for being a stock swap transaction or for having real synergies. Furthermore, the Bayer-Monsanto deal was considered, but declined due to the higher P/E of Monsanto compared to Bayer.[62,63]

Nevertheless, the exemplary calculation illustrates the importance of a profound analysis to evaluate a business. The SVN and the SHV represent a suitable approach to evaluate long-team investment strategies suchlike M&A transactions. The shortcomings of the P/E, EPS and other multiples are underlined by the bootstrap effect as well as their short-term orientation. A decent business evaluation should integrate long-term oriented calculation methods as the SHV does through the discounted cash flow and WACC. According to Rappaport,[64] there are certain principles managers should follow to create shareholder value in long-term orientation and not in quarterly steps. Executives should orient themselves on the maximisation of shareholder value, even if this means the lowering of near-term earnings. Therefore, justifying strategies and acquisitions on a short-term EPS increase is not beneficial to create a sustainable and long-living business dedicated to shareholder value maximisation.

5 Conclusion

Summarizing, M&A have a significant influence on stock prices. Even before a transaction is closed and the takeover is proceeded an impact is traceable. Announcing takeover entail changes of the target's and the acquirer's stock prices, whereas targets have more gains compared to acquirers. Overall, M&A are mostly beneficial for the involved entities; if the reasons for the transaction are long-term oriented and realistic synergies exist.

Efficient markets will eliminate the short-term gains from the bootstrap effect. Thus, a viable and straightforward strategy for the entire business is the best value driver managers should comply with, to maximise shareholder value. The shareholder value network and its value drivers represent a still appropriate management approach to meet today's challenges of fast-paced changes. Its universal and cross-industry applicability allows management to decide on strategic decisions concerning operations, investment or financing.

---

[61] CB Insights, „Fools Rush In: 27 Of The Worst Corporate M&A Flops," October 6, 2016, https://www.cbinsights.com/blog/merger-acquisition-corporate-fails/, accessed July 2017.

[62] Yahoo! Finance, "Bayer Aktiengesellschaft (BAYN.DE)," https://finance.yahoo.com/quote/MON?p=MON, accessed July 2017.

[63] Yahoo! Finance, "Monsanto Company (MON)," https://finance.yahoo.com/quote/BAYN.DE?p=BAYN.DE, accessed July 2017.

[64] Rappaport, Alfred, "Ten Ways to Create Shareholder Value".

Besides this, M&A as well as the business as a whole can be evaluated by the approach. This leads to a continuing business optimisation due to the derived potential savings and consolidations creating shareholder value.

Annex

A-1: Weighted average cost of capital

The WACC is calculated as shown below:[65]

$$r_{wacc} = \frac{E}{E+D} r_E + \frac{D}{E+D} r_D (1 - \tau_C)$$

(3)

E = value of equity

r_E = equity cost of capital

D = value of debt

r_D = debt cost of capital

τ_C = corporate tax rate

---

[65] Berk, J., and Peter DeMarzo, *Corporate Finance*, p. 422.

A-2: Free cash flow

The free cash flow is calculated as follows:[66]

    Sales

    − Cost of goods sold

    = <u>Gross profit</u>

    − Selling, general, and administrative (SG&A) expenses

    − Research and development (R&D)

    − Depreciation

    = <u>Earnings before interest and taxes (EBIT)</u>

    − Income Tax

    = <u>Unlevered Net Income</u>

    + Depreciation

    − Capital expenditures

    − Increase in net working capital (NWC)

    = <u>Free Cash Flow (FCF)</u>   (4)

---

[66] Berk, J., and Peter DeMarzo, *Corporate Finance*, p. 241.

A-3: Earnings per share and price-earnings ratio

EPS is calculated if the shares outstanding divide the net income. Net income is the deduction of the interests and taxes from the EBIT. Calculation of the earnings per share:[67]

$$EPS = \frac{Net\ Income}{Shares\ Outstanding} \tag{5}$$

Calculation of the price-earnings ratio:[68]

$$P/E\ Ratio = \frac{Market\ Capitalization}{Net\ Income} = \frac{Share\ Price}{Earnings\ per\ Share} \tag{6}$$

To calculate the correct post-merger P/E ratio, the pre-merger P/E ratios must be weighted, which will prevent the bootstrap effect. Calculation as follows:[69]

$$P/E\ Ratio = \frac{(P_A \times S_A) + (P_B \times S_B)}{E_A + E_B} \tag{7}$$

P_A, P_B = pre-merger share price of Company A, B

S_A, S_B = number of outstanding shares of Company A, B

E_A, E_B = earnings of Company A, B

---

[67] Berk, J., and Peter DeMarzo, *Corporate Finance*, p. 30.
[68] Ibid., p. 41.
[69] Gaughan, Patrick A., *Mergers, Acquisitions and Corporate Restructuring*, pp. 540-541.

Bibliography

Berk, J., and Peter DeMarzo. *Corporate Finance*, 3rd ed. Boston, MA: Pearson, 2014.

Brealey, Richard A., Myers, Stewart C., and Alan J. Marcus. *Fundamentals of Corporate Finance*, 3rd ed. McGraw-Hill Higher Education, 2001.

Brealey, Richard A., Myers, Stewart C., and Franklin Allen. *Principles of Corporate Finance*, 10th ed. Boston, MA: McGraw-Hill/Irwin, 2011.

Chari, Latha, and R. P. Mohanty. "Understanding Value Creation: The Shareholder Value Perspective." *LBS Journal of Management & Research* 7, no. 1 and 2 (2009), pp. 12 - 26.

Gantenbein, P. and M. Gehrig. "Moderne Unternehmensbewertung - Bewertungsziel mit Methodenmix erreichen." Der Schweizer Treuhänder 9 (2007), pp. 602 - 612.

Gaughan, Patrick A. *Mergers, Acquisitions and Corporate Restructuring*, 3rd ed. New York, John Wiley & Sons, 2002.

Giurca, Vasilecu Laura. "New Approaches On Shareholders Value Of A Firm." Faculty of Economy and Business Administration, University of Craiova, 2007, pp. 662-666.

Lohr, Burkhard. *Bewertung bauausführender Unternehmen: Ein ganzheitliches entscheidungsorientiertes Konzept.* Munich: Herbert Utz Verlag, 2001.

McGowan, Carl B., and Zunaidah Sulong. "A Note On The Effect Of M&A Announcements On Stock Price Behavior And Financial Performance Changes: The Case Of Arab Malaysian Bank Berhad And Hong Leong Bank Berhad." *International Business & Economics Research Journal* 7, no. 9 (September 2008), pp. 21-26.

Kumar, B. Rajesh, and S. Panneerselvam. "Mergers, Acquisitions and Wealth Creation: A Comparative Study in the Indian Context." *IIMB Management Review* 21, no. 3 (2009), pp. 222-244.

Pandey, M., and D. Arora. "Shareholder Value Analysis: A Review." *International Journal of Science and Research* 4, no. 5 (May 2015), pp. 2129-2132.

Pike, Richard, and Bill Neale. *Corporate Finance and Investment: Decisions & Strategies*, 5th ed. Harlow: Financial Times Prentice Hall, 2006.

Prangenberg, Arno, Müller, Matthias, and Manuela Aldenhoff. "Der Shareholder-Value-Ansatz." *Arbeitshilfen für Aufsichtsräte* 9, 4th ed. Düsseldorf: Hans-Böckler-Stiftung, 2005.

Rappaport, Alfred. *Creating Shareholder Value: A Guide For Managers and Investors.* New York, NY: The Free Press, 1998.

Ross, Stephen A., Westerfield, Randolph W., and Jaffrey Jaffe. *Corporate Finance*, 6th ed. Boston, MA: McGraw-Hill/Irwin, 2003.

Wellner, Kai-Uwe. *Shareholder-Value und seine Weiterentwicklung zum Market Adapted Shareholder Value Approach.* Marburg: Tectum Verlag, 2001.

Wong, Anson, and Kui Yin Cheung. "The Effects of Merger and Acquisition Announcements on the Security Prices of Bidding Firms and Target Firms in Asia." *International Journal of Economics and Finance* 1, no. 2 (August 2009), pp. 274-283.

Internet bibliography

AmerisourceBergen.   "SEC   Filings   –   AmerisourceBergen."
  http://www.amerisourcebergen.net/investor/phoenix.zhtml?c=61181&p=irol-
  SECText&TEXT=aHR0cDovL2FwaS50ZW5rd2l6YXJkLmNvbS9maWxpcP2lw
  YWdlPTE0NDY3MTYmRFNFUT0wJlNFUT0wJlNRREVTQz1TRUNUSU9OX0VOVEl5
  RSZzdWJzaWQ9NTc%3d, accessed June 2017.
CB Insights. „Fools Rush In: 27 Of The Worst Corporate M&A Flops." October 6, 2016.
  https://www.cbinsights.com/blog/merger-acquisition-corporate-fails/, accessed July
  2017.
CFA Institute, "Chapter 10 – Mergers and Acquisitions," PowerPoint presentation, 2013,
  https://www.cfainstitute.org/learning/products/publications/inv/Documents/corporate_fi
  nance_chapter10.pptx, accessed July 2017.
Mergermarket.   "Global   and   regional   M&A: Q1-Q4   2016."
  [http://www.mergermarket.com/pdf/MergermarketFinancialLeagueTableReport.Q4201
  6.pdf], accessed April 2017.
Rappaport, Alfred. "Ten Ways to Create Shareholder Value." Harvard Business Review, September 2006. https://hbr.org/2006/09/ten-ways-to-create-shareholder-value, accessed
  July 2017.
Reckard, E. Scott, and Leslie Earnest. "Bergen Agrees to Be Acquired by AmeriSource in
  $2.3-Billion Deal." Los Angeles Times, March 20, 2001.
  http://articles.latimes.com/2001/mar/20/business/fi-40082, accessed July 2017.
Yahoo!   Finance.   "Bayer   Aktiengesellschaft   (BAYN.DE)."
  https://finance.yahoo.com/quote/MON?p=MON, accessed July 2017.
Yahoo!   Finance.   "Monsanto   Company   (MON)."
  https://finance.yahoo.com/quote/BAYN.DE?p=BAYN.DE, accessed July 2017.

YOUR KNOWLEDGE HAS VALUE

- We will publish your bachelor's and
  master's thesis, essays and papers

- Your own eBook and book -
  sold worldwide in all relevant shops

- Earn money with each sale

Upload your text at www.GRIN.com
and publish for free